Lambeth and Liturgy 1988

The Lambeth 1988 Statement on Liturgy

Edited with Introduction and Commentary

by

Colin Buchanan

Bishop of Aston; Secretary of the Lambeth Conference 'Renewal in Liturgy' working group

GROVE BOOKS LIMITED

Bramcote   Nottingham   NG9 3DS

CONTENTS

ACKNOWLEDGMENTS

All the Lambeth materials reproduced here are published by kind permission of the Secretary-General of the Anglican Consultative Council and Secretary of the Lambeth Conference, Canon Sam Van Culin. I am particularly grateful to him (and to Mr. Robin Brookes of Church House Publishing) for their helpfulness in enabling me to see the Lambeth Conference report in proof in order to ensure accuracy of reproduction and swiftness of publication. In presentation of the text, I have altered the form of the cross-headings, followed my own house-style, and corrected official misprints (in three places drawing attention to a change of meaning thus imported). I should add that there is no comment here on the worship *at* the Lambeth Conference. No-one other than the writer is bound by any statements or sentiments deriving solely from me.

COB January 1989

THE COVER PICTURE

is by permission adapted from the logo of the Lambeth Conference

THE LAMBETH 'RENEWAL IN LITURGY' WORKING GROUP

Bishop Roger Herft, Bp. of Waikato, New Zealand—Chairman
Bishop Abraham Awosan, Bp. of Owo, Nigeria
Bishop Fraser Berry, Bp. of Kootenay, Chairman of the Doctrine and Worship Committee of
    the Anglican Church of Canada
Bishop David Birney, Bp. of Idaho, Episcopal Church of the USA
Bishop Colin Buchanan, Bp. of Aston, Church of England—Secretary[1]
Bishop Rex Donat, Bp. of Mauritius, Indian Ocean
Bishop Colin James, Bp. of Winchester, Chairman of the Church of England Liturgical
    Commission
Bishop Edward Luscombe, Bp. of Brechin, Primus of the Scottish Episcopal Church
Bishop Dinis Sengulane, Bp. of Lebombo, Mozambique, Southern Africa
Bishop John Stewart, Bp. of Western Region of Melbourne, Australia

First Impression January 1989

ISSN 0144-1728
ISBN 1 85174 094 5

[1] I became secretary largely because, being from England, I was able to bring a fair library of Anglican liturgical books and reports with me; and I also brought a word processor to Canterbury, and thus was ready to re-draft painlessly between sessions. Whilst the group secretary *may* have thus had certain opportunities to initiate the contents of the statement and to shape its presentation, he was nevertheless subject to very close scrutiny by the group, and claims that, *qua* scribe, he acted solely as the group's servant.

1. INTRODUCTION—THE LAMBETH CONFERENCE 1988

Lambeth Conferences are held every ten years. They have no authoritative status within the Anglican Communion, but are, in the strictest terms, simply and literally 'conferences' of those Anglican bishops whom the Archbishop of Canterbury chooses to invite. The Anglican Communion itself has traditionally been a strictly indefinable concept, and until the first Lambeth Conference it was extremely shadowy as a concept. Then from 1867 to 1968 it could only be defined as a family of episcopal Churches whose bishops are, as described above, invited to the Lambeth Conferences by the Archbishops of Canterbury.[1] And the discretion of the Archbishop of Canterbury still governs both the membership of the Conference itself and the other categories of persons attending. The episcopal membership, for instance, in 1988 included all diocesan bishops, and a proportion of suffragan and assistant bishops. Other Lambeth Conferences have included no suffragans or a different proportion of them. The other participants in 1988 included the whole Anglican Consultative Council, which was not the case in 1978.[2] And similarly the range of consultants and observers also differed in 1988 from previous occasions.

The Process

The upshot was that around 525 bishops took part in the three-week Conference at the University of Kent in Canterbury from 17 July to 7 August 1988. These 525 at intervals met in plenary session, and all resolutions of the Conference were adopted in plenary. They also met in four separate sections, entitled 'Mission and Ministry', 'Dogmatic and Pastoral', 'Ecumenical Relations' and 'Church and Society'. The sub-division of the work to be done by each section was indicated in broad outline through a preparatory working party which met at Blackheath in South-East London in August 1987 and produced in a report sub-headings for each of the sections and brief summaries of the ground to be covered under each sub-heading. In 'Mission and Ministry' there was a sub-heading 'Renewal of the Church for its Mission' and under that there were four further sub-divisions: 'Charismatic Renewal', 'Renewal in Liturgy', 'Theological Renewal' and 'Transformation'. In general, those coming to the Lambeth Conference had already opted for one of the four main themes, but there was some scope for further choosing of the particular subject which interested any particular bishop, and thus the actual group which worked on 'Renewal in Liturgy' was partly self-selecting, and partly accidental. A 'group' was around ten persons, meeting largely as a group to write a draft statement within the first two weeks of the three-week period. At intervals the group reported to the section which had generally to approve its drafting, and incorporate it into a larger statement from the whole section.

[1] Historically, this point has been well made. In 1867 itself Colenso, Bishop of Natal, about whose continuance in office after deposition by his 'metropolitan' the whole first Lambeth Conference was being convened, was not invited by Archbishop Longley. In 1958 Fred Morris, Bishop of the Church of England in South Africa (which in some ways claimed the legal succession from the first Anglican communities in South Africa) was not invited by Archbishop Fisher, who thus declared that particular episcopal church, headed by an undoubted 'Anglican' bishop, *not* part of the Anglican Communion—and by definition there was no appeal. Since 1968 the Anglican Communion has had a more formal federal 'instrument' of identity—the Anglican Consultative Council which first met in 1971. See also footnote 2 following.

[2] In 1988, the ACC members were present at Archbishop Runcie's own discretion (though he certainly sought and obtained advice). This had not been the case in 1978, a contrast which further illustrates the point made in footnote 1 above.

3

The Group at Work

Such was the plan for working. The group which found itself working on 'Renewal in the Liturgy' is listed on the 'Contents' page above. It was almost identical with the group which met after breakfast each day for an hour's Bible-study, sharing and prayer.[1] The warmth and mutual relationships which developed then became an important context for the drafting work done later in the day. And the group was quickly seized with the importance of its task, for giving true leadership in the Anglican Communion.

Oddly, although the preparatory Blackheath group a year before had identified the subject of 'Renewal in Liturgy' as a component feature of the 'Mission and Ministry' agenda, the actual outline it had produced of the liturgical task was scrappy, brief, and almost irrelevant. Thus when the group met on the first Wednesday, it virtually began from scratch. The only other resource given it was the Belfast report.[2] However, the secretary was asked to prepare something substantial immediately for reflection the next day. Whilst this unguided work was greatly changed by the time of the eighth draft near the end of the Conference, the existence of an original draft against which to think focussed minds helpfully.

The group quickly realized that their work must be achieved in the context of the work on 'mission' to which the section as a whole was addressing itself. It also became clear how the immediate liturgical agendas of the different countries represented at the Conference varied as between various parts of the world. Anything drafted had to stand up in Nigeria, Mozambique, Mauritius, New Zealand and Scotland! And the group was also visited by experts from outside its membership, of whom the first two were official Consultants, and the third a bishop from another group.[3] During the process the third draft went to a section meeting on the second Monday, and from then on the group had six further group meetings to reach a final draft, more or less agreed by the section during the third week.

From Section to Publication

The section meetings of around 130 bishops were highly unsatisfactory, as lengthy drafts came to people who had not previously digested them and were unacquainted with the rationale or particular careful discussion which lay behind the tabled text. The section was short of time for proper presentation, and thus on the one hand whole chunks went through with little probing, whilst on the other the mildest of reforms could be suddenly subject to a snap vote and be deleted by a narrow majority.[4]

[1] One lay member of the ACC and one other American bishop were part of the Bible-study group but not of the drafting group, and Bishop Dinis Sengulane, a member of a different Bible-study group, joined with the rest for the drafting task.

[2] The report of the international Anglican conference of young people at Belfast in January 1988 is entitled *Love in any Language*, and all drafting groups were asked to take it into account, and two delegates from Belfast took part as consultants in the Lambeth Conference. In fact, its treatment of 'Mission and Ministry' hardly mentioned worship.

[3] These were Stephen Sykes (of the Church of England); Janet Hodgson (of Southern Africa) and Ted Eastman (of USA). Of these, the first wanted a common set of forms, rather on the 1662 model, which would undergird the Anglican Communion's identity. This the group would not concede. The second thought that the drafting had somehow missed the point on inculturation, but declined to suggest other forms of words—whilst the group thought it had made the point forcefully enough and was content with its own thrust. The third was satisfied with the treatment of baptism and the catechumenate.

[4] Odd snap actions by the section are recorded below as, e.g., in footnote 2 opposite.

By mid-way through the third week there was no further opportunity for group re-drafting, and the whole task fell into the hands of the section secretary, Bishop Pat Harris, who had just completed a term as the secretary of the Church of England's Partnership in World Mission and was being appointed Bishop of Southwell. He kept in touch with group secretaries, and took a decision of principle to incorporate the liturgical material into the section statement not by including it in the place it had been supposed to come, but, because of its length and detail, to place it after the other material, as a distinct piece of writing, with a cross-reference to it in the main text.[1] He then passed the 'Mission and Ministry' drafting on, a day or two after the Conference finished, to Bishop Michael Nazir Ali and Mr. Derek Pattinson, who were to take responsibility for the final editing of the text. They not only brought some consistency to the whole presentation of the section statements, but added footnotes for the sake of cross-referencing and noting sources. In the liturgy section they occasionally added material which I doubt whether the original group would have accepted—at least in the form in which it was added—and I have mentioned that in the Commentary below at such points. The historical introduction to this section disappeared again, and I have printed it here instead as chapter 2, virtually as originally drafted.

After the editing together into a single report of the section statements along with the resolutions and other Lambeth material, the final product was duly published on 16 January 1989 as *The Truth Shall Make You Free: The Lambeth Conference 1988* (Church House Publishing for the ACC, 1989), with the liturgy portion of the statements as paragraphs 175-207.

The Resolutions

Each group could bring draft resolutions to its section, and have them forwarded from there for debate and voting by the plenary Conference in the final week. In addition to this, 'private members' could also table resolutions for plenary adoption. The 500-plus bishops meeting in plenary were desperately handicapped by pressures of time, by lack of standing orders and some cavalier chairmanship, and sheer lack of resources and preparation for dealing with the worldwide range of issues which came in bewildering succession for instant decision in plenary.

Six resolutions with some liturgical reference came before the plenaries. These are set out, with a brief commentary on each, on pages 24-25 below. Only one of these, no.47, originated from the group, and the other five came from different sections, or from private members.[2]

The Status of the Statement and Resolutions

Lambeth Conferences have no legislative power, and thus their utterances have no weight any greater than the internal force of their contents on the one hand and the expertise and credibility of their authors on the other.

[1] Curiously, this possibility had been raised when the liturgy group had first reported to the section. Then, however, it had been deemed right to keep the material as short as possible, in order to include it *within* the main statement without unbalancing the contents too greatly. In particular, the historical introduction which had been drafted was set aside as not fitting the context. However, now that the liturgical material was to come *after* the main statement, there was a case for re-introducing the historical introduction.

[2] No. 69 arose from an original draft by the group on liturgy, but this was suddenly excised by the section, and, after some further softening of its terms, was, with the goodwill of the section, then submitted by Archbishop Brian Davis of New Zealand in his own person.

2. SOME HISTORICAL BACKGROUND

The Lambeth Conference of 1958 included in its reports a thorough review of 'The Book of Common Prayer' conducted by a sub-committee considering 'Progress in the Anglican Communion'. This report was the first ever from a Lambeth Conference not to insist that the traditional (Cranmer-style) Book of Common Prayer (varying slightly from 1662 in some Provinces) was a great component of common Anglican identity. Instead, before many of the changes now taken for granted had even broken surface, the 1958 bishops boldly addressed themselves to a changing future. They set out some principles, looked closely at baptism, eucharist, and ordination, touched on many other issues, and thus put down markers which have been of great (though not equal) value in the three decades since.

There has been no serious handling of liturgical issues on a pan-Anglican basis on the same scale since that 1958 report. Arising from its report (2.81, Resolution 76) a small committee produced a short document on 'The Structure and Contents of the Eucharistic Liturgy' in 1965.[1] This was revised slightly and re-published in 1969 at the request of a post-Lambeth Liturgical Consultation held in 1968.[2] The 1968 Lambeth Conference itself did not consider liturgy, save for a recommendation of experiments about initiation (in the 'Ministry' section p.99), apparently in order to facilitate a commissioning of the lay Christian at the age of adult responsibility.[3] Lambeth 1978 included a brief report of a group which had worked on the issue of lay presidency at the eucharist (p.83), and a brief and very general review of worship around the Anglican Communion (pp.94-95). Resolution 23 asked for the ACC to be responsible for acting as a 'clearing-house' for liturgical information across the Communion and Resolution 24 recommended a common lectionary.

The Anglican Consultative Council itself has given little space to discussing liturgy, though ACC-2 report (1973) included a specially prepared report on 'Liturgy 1968-1973' and ACC-6 (1984) followed this by commissioning a report on 'Liturgy 1973-1984'. This was circulated to members in advance with a short document from the Primates' meeting of October 1983 entitled 'How does the Anglican Communion retain its traditional sense of unity?' These two documents were not published in the report of ACC-6, but have been since.[4] 'Liturgy 1973-84' drew attention to the fact that ecumenical discussions (and particularly ARCIC, though it would have been true of the discussion of the Lima text) were reflecting on the eucharist without reference to the various liturgical texts of the parties concerned, and that this was potentially dangerous.

---

[1] It was printed with an introduction in Colin Buchanan (ed.) *Modern Anglican Liturgies 1958-1968* (Oxford, 1968) pp.22-32.

[2] It was printed in Colin Buchanan (ed.) *Further Anglican Liturgies 1968-1975* (Grove Books, Nottingham, 1975) pp.26-31.

[3] Resolution 25 (on page 37 of the report), which gives formal expression to this, is cited by Archbishop Brian Davis as that which gave 'stimulus for reform' leading to the admission of young unconfirmed children to communion in New Zealand (see his 'New Zealand Initiation Experience' in Colin Buchanan (ed.) *Nurturing Children in Communion: Essays from the Boston Consultation* (Grove Books, Nottingham, 1985) p.23.

[4] They form an appendix in Colin Buchanan *Anglican Eucharistic Liturgy 1975-1985* (Grove Liturgical Study no. 41, 1985) pp.24-32.

In 1983, at the end of the biennial Congress of *Societas Liturgica* in Vienna, a few Anglicans present resolved to meet as Anglicans for a Consultation prior to the Boston (Mass.) Congress of *Societas* due in 1985. This Consultation met by invitation from its founding chairman and secretary (Canon Donald Gray and Professor David Holeton) and twelve persons present considered questions about admission to communion, and prepared a 'Boston Statement' which unanimously called upon the Anglican Provinces to admit to communion on the basis of baptism only.[1]

A second Consultation was planned to follow the next meeting of *Societas Liturgica* in Northern Italy in August 1987. ACC-7, at its meeting in May 1987, took note of this and recorded Resolution 11 (p.73):

'THAT this Council:

(a) recognizes the 1987 Consultation, which is not to be funded by the ACC, and requests that its proceedings be made available to the ACC and the Lambeth Conference 1988

(b) recommends that the membership of future Consultations be widely representative of the Communion, and that the Secretary-General be requested to confer with the organizers aboput its future meetings;

(c) encourages Provinces to give financial support for members of their Province who attend such gatherings.'

ACC-7 also considered the Boston material somewhat hesitantly (pp.68-70, including a prejudicial photo, not commissioned by the ACC(!), and Resolution 10): and it also recommended, in Resolution 12, the creation of an 'Anglican Communion Liturgical Commission'.[2]

The second Consultation duly met at Brixen, received a letter from the Archbishop of Canterbury commending its expected work, and also learned of Resolutions 10,11, and 12 of ACC-7. Its work took two forms: in part the sixteen members responded negatively to the concept of an Anglican Communion Liturgical Commission and agreed instead the 'Brixen Submission'. In part they gave themselves to considering prepared papers on 'Liturgical Formation'.[3]

A third Anglican Liturgical Consultation is being planned to follow the next meeting of *Societas Liturgica* at York in August 1989. Meanwhile the ACC Standing Committee has met in November 1988, and has given further recognition to the successive Consultations, without taking action about a Commission.

[1] The papers associated with this were published (see reference in footnote 3 on page 6 opposite), and the Statement itself was included in this Symposium also. Copies were supplied to ACC-7, which met in Singapore in May 1987. (See paragraph 192 on page 16 below, and Resolution 69 on page 24, and the attached Commentaries
[2] See paragraph 176 and Commentary, pp.10-11 below.
[3] These are now published as Thomas Talley (ed.) *A Kingdom of Priests: Liturgical Formation of the People of God* (Alcuin/GROW Joint Liturgical Study 5, Grove Books, 1988), with an offshoot published as Colin Buchanan (ed.) *The Bishop in Liturgy: An Anglican Symposium on the Role and Task of the Bishop in the Field of Liturgy* (Alcuin/GROW Joint Liturgical Study 6, Grove Books, 1988).

3. THE STATEMENT—TEXT

[Paragraphs 59 and 177-209 of the 'Mission and Ministry' Statement]

RENEWAL OF THE CHURCH IN LITURGY[1]

59. The renewal of the Church for its mission is intimately bound up with its worship. We seek that our worship should in fact, by the power of the Spirit, bring renewal to the Church. But we are also aware that more specific guidance on the subject of liturgy might, for all our purpose of mission, apppear somewhat inward-looking and over-concerned with detail if set out in full here. We therefore provide a fuller discussion of worship as the last section of the Report (paras. 177-209), and recommend that it be both studied there and taken into account in the developing argument of our statement here.

_____

THE RENEWAL OF THE CHURCH IN LITURGY

177. Although the Anglican Consultative Council has given *some* consideration to liturgical matters at various meetings, it is thirty years since a Lambeth Conference gave any extensive guidance on liturgical matters. Since 1958 there has been great liturgical change. Texts have been revised and modernized all over the world. Vatican II has touched us all. The Liturgical Movement has reshaped Sunday, the eucharist, and even church interiors. Also it has significantly reshaped the mentalities and expectations of the worshippers as well. Around us the world to which we are sent has changed astonishingly also, as other parts of this statement reflect. It is time to consider the worship of the Church afresh.

The Heart of Worship
178. Christian worship has its own self-authenticating character as the prime duty of the Church of God. It should be offered to God by the Church for his glory and without any conscious eye to some other ulterior purpose. The mystery of worship is that the Church is caught up into the heavens, so as to be forgetful of herself and simply to gaze on the vision of God.

Worship and Mission
179. Yet it is also true that in worship the Church should so re-discover both herself and God's purposes for her, every member should so meet God and the people of God, that through the rhythm of the Church's worshipping life all are richly equipped for service in the world. The Church's liturgy, thus, is bound up with her mission, and the renewal of her liturgy is bound up with the renewal of her mission.

[1] Paragraph 59 is included as a trailer, and is only covered here by this footnote, rather than by 'Commentary'. All other footnotes on left-hand pages are footnotes *to* the statement itself, added by the statement's editors (see pages 4 and 5 above). Paragraph 59 represents the place in the structure of the whole statement where, if the 'Blackheath' plan had been followed faithfully, a brief statement on worship would have fitted. As it was, the length of the work on liturgy presented a problem—and originally, as prepared by the group, it was longer still. The group had in mind all along that it might have to go in the middle (i.e. here at 59), and they trimmed it carefully. The section and its secretary then decided to put it at the end notwithstanding, and to include only this cross-referencing paragraph at the place indicated. 59 emphasizes the need to see the liturgical part of the statement, however long, and however remotely placed, as part of the whole, taking its place here at 59 within the argument.

4. COMMENTARY ON THE STATEMENT

Paragraph 177 introduces the separate section on worship, to which 59 cross-refers. The opening sentence is the last footprint of a background section, originally drafted by the group, which set out a history of pan-Anglican decision-taking on worship since Lambeth 1958. This drafting is now reproduced as chapter 2 above. Michael Nazir Ali added a few footnotes to the whole statement to make up for the lack of historical background, and the first sentence of 177 also expresses this.

The Lambeth Conference Statement of 1958 was a notable milestone. 1958 was the first time that it had been acknowledged that liturgical revision might be either necesary or beneficial—and thus it was the first time that the unity of liturgical ethos afforded by the 1662 BCP and its near relations was recognized as departing. The Anglican Communion started to face up to its liturgical future.[1] On the other hand most of the emphasis lay upon the revision of *texts*, and little upon the updating of the style of worship—and even in the field of texts, no-one in 1958 could have contemplated the changes afoot, such as that within ten years the axe would be laid to the root of the tree of Cranmer's liturgical English.

The references to Vatican II and to the Liturgical Movement also give an historical context. The Vatican Constitution on the Sacred Liturgy was promulged in December 1963, and, from a Roman Catholic point of view, both gave expression to the progress of the Liturgical Movement and also gave that progress a tremendous extra momentum. Here the emphasis is more upon 'style' than upon texts in the narrow sense.[2] The Liturgical Movement has sought a wholeness in the liturgy which is only incidentally exhibited in the texts. The participation and comprehension of all the people; the building of Christian community; the expression before God of the faith and concerns of *this* people—these are the themes of the Liturgical Movement. They do in passing entail and stimulate reform of texts: but they switch the main attention from the texts and textual revision.

The Lambeth Statement mirrors this sense of priorities. Whilst all round the world Anglicans are revising liturgical texts, that was not the chief concern of this pan-Anglican Statement. There is virtually no reference to the particularities of liturgical texts, and at the same time there is great weight placed upon general liturgical principles.

Paragraph 178 is self-explanatory—a timely reminder of the eternal prior to discussion of all the temporal features of the liturgical events.

Paragraph 179 highlights the place of 'Renewal of the Church in Liturgy' within the 'Mission and Ministry' section of the Conference. In one sense, it is in tension with the previous paragraph, as the planning and execution of liturgical events must, on this analysis, be very concerned for their effect upon the worshippers. The group faced this tension, knowing that the Church's self-forgetfulness set out in paragraph 178 must inevitably lead into a self-consciousness, not, we hope, confined to its navel, but much more focussed on its mission. Part of the key to mission is *meeting* and, in the presence of God, strengthening each other's hands. The liturgy itself now has a strong reference to the work and witness of the members outside of the liturgy—conceived in general terms as 'service'.

[1] See *The Lambeth Conference 1958*, 2.78-98.

[2] The Roman Catholic Church has of course proceeded to revise its liturgical texts in an astonishingly radical way. But that goes far beyond the programme built into the Constitution on the Sacred Liturgy.

The Universality of Worship

180. The catholicity of the visible Church must be expressed in some common forms and rituals. The people of God are joined together in one Body by baptism and faith. By the power of the Holy Spirit they continue in the body through sharing the eucharist, through dependence upon God's word, through fellowship in prayer, service, and suffering. In our Communion we expect that proper regard to these catholic features of worship will be paid in a responsible way by all our Provinces. In principle, we commend all means of communication and co-ordination in respect of liturgy between our Provinces, while not wishing to compromise their proper constitutional autonomy.

In this respect we note the ACC-7 resolution concerning the creation of an International Anglican Liturgical Commission. We request that the Standing Committee of ACC, when it next meets, considers carefully how such a Commission could actually fulfil the hopes being placed upon it.[26]

Local Expression of the Liturgy

181. The liturgy of the Church must ever draw upon the past and conserve the best of the tradition. In particular it must enshrine and hand on the work [*misprint for* 'word'] of God, in the written liturgical texts, in the lectionary provision, and in a vigorous pattern of preaching and teaching. These provide much of the spiritual resources by which the Church lives in the world. Yet the liturgy must at the same time give authentic expression to the common life in Christ of the people of God present at each particular gathering, in whatever generation and in whatever country and culture (cf. Article 34 of the Thirty-nine Articles).

182. Thus, for instance, the hymnody of each place and time will both express the timeless and universal Word of God and express it in a poetic and musical form appropriate to the worshippers. Hymnody and Christian singing generally are an instance of a marvellous means of worship, a great channel of the truths of God, an expression of faith and joy which springs from the heart of the worshippers—and yet one open to the possibility of fossilization if the times move on and the music and singing slowly become that of a cultural ghetto. The Church has to worship incarnationally, separated from the world by the offence of the cross, but not by any alien character of its culture. We affirm expressions of true local creativity within the life of the worshipping local community which well up from within the people in response to the stirrings of the Spirit. Thus we commend and encourage authentic local inculturation of the liturgy, and fear lest in many parts of the Anglican Communion we have been all too hesitant about it.

Liturgy Comes Alive

183. Authorized liturgical forms embody doctrine, and the stance of faith of each Province is in part discerned from its liturgical forms. Such forms, nevertheless, provide but a part of the actual event of the liturgy, and the totality will usually include scripture reading, hymnody, locally devised forms of intercession, preaching or other communication, movement (e.g. at the Peace or during the

[26] *Many Gifts, One Spirit,* pp.74-76.

Paragraph 180 sets out certain universal features of the liturgy—a necessary background to the thoroughgoing commendation of local 'inculturation' and adaptation which is to come in the next paragraphs. The Anglican Communion cannot of course *enforce* uniformity, nor, in the last analysis, over-rule an autonomous Province which decides to take a path of brinkmanship (or worse) in its liturgical uses.[1] But the Lambeth Conference has some reason to hope that its general principles here will hold, and equally has good reason to treat each Province as 'responsible'.

The second part of paragraph 180 touches on a particular matter of a slightly specialized character. The ACC Resolution in May 1987 called for this Commission. The Brixen International Anglican Liturgical Consultation made a 'Submission' asking the ACC not to do it that way, and the Submission was made available to the drafting group. Some of the problems raised by the Commission idea were aired at Lambeth (particularly the questions as to whether it would be permanent or not, and as to *how* it would respond to a steady stream of enquiries from round the Anglican world), and it was agreed that the English members of the group would meet with Sam Van Culin, Colin Craston and Donald Gray before the ACC Standing Committee met in November 1988, and work through the 'Commission-versus-Consultations' issue.[2] That meeting took place just before the Standing Committee of ACC met, and weighed up the ACC-7 recommendation, the Brixen 'Submission', and the 'Advisory Body' sought by Lambeth Resolution 18. When the Standing Committee itself met, it took no action about a Commission.

Paragraphs 181 and 182 begin by repeating the 'catholic' features of the Church's liturgy, but go on to urge true 'inculturation' and readiness for constant further adaptation (in the outward form of the liturgy) to changing times. There has been a suspicion around of liturgical colonialism, whereby the younger Churches were confined to the nineteenth century uses of English or American parishes. The group's statement (drafted with vastly differing parts of the world represented in the group and section) shows that the identity and unity of the Anglican Communion cannot now be thought to be bound up with a single identifiable liturgical usage.[3]

Paragraph 183 is a warning to Anglicans lest they equate the substance of worship with written liturgical texts. Worship is a function of *people*, and thus varies considerably from one congregation to another, even when the programme in the book is identical in both. Furthermore, the other physical ingredients (where the paragraph might also, for the sake of the argument, have included incense, though in fact it did not) can also vary enormously even whilst the same textual programme is being followed. A worship event is complex, and true understanding of it involves all the dimensions concerned. A truly participatory ethos reflects the Liturgical Movement emphases—necessary for that 'building up' of the people of God.

[1] Even the 'policing' Resolution 18 (see p.24 below) could not actually *enforce* anything.
[2] Colin Craston is the English member of the ACC Standing Committee (and originator of the Commission notion) and was present at Lambeth as ACC member: Donald Gray was chairman of the Brixen Consultation. (It should be noted that, as with the 'policing' motion, ACC may not have funds for such a Commission anyway . . .)
[3] 'Inculturation' was a theme at Brixen too—see the chapter by Elisha Mbonigaba in Thomas Talley (ed.) *A Kingdom of Priests: The Liturgical Formation of the Laity* (Alcuin/GROW Joint Liturgical Study no. 5, Grove Books, Nottingham, 1988) and the post-Lambeth Phillip Tovey *Inculturation of the Liturgy: The Eucharist in Africa* (Alcuin/GROW Joint Liturgical Study no. 7, Grove Books, Nottingham, 1988). The same emphasis is to be found in Resolutions 22 and 47 on page 24 below.

administration of communion), and silence. In addition to these, the actual 'ethos' of worship is determined also by the number and disposition of the participants, by the buildings, furnishings, art, ornamentation, vesture, musical resources and ceremonial associated with the particular liturgical event. A welcome trend is towards much fuller active participation by the congregation, and this helps us conceive of liturgy as a function of living people actually participating in an *event*. Worship involves the people of the Spirit worshipping in spirit and in truth, and we must not equate it solely with texts, however scriptural and commendable, on the pages of a book.

1662 and other Prayer Books

184. The 1662 Book of Common Prayer of the Church of England, and along with it the other Prayer Books of the Anglican Communion, have been hugely influential in shaping the identity of the Communion as a seriously liturgical fellowship of Churches. The 1662 Prayer Book, in particular, has been influential not only in England but in many other parts of the world as well. In some Provinces, especially where it is used in a local vernacular tongue, it still feeds people with a secure spirituality; and in these and other Provinces it often remains as a standard of doctrine. But if we do not dwell on its *strengths* to-day it is because we judge its era is slipping irretrievably into the past. Cranmer's liturgical language is that of another age—though we recognize this is not always the case in translation into other languages.

185. The presuppositions of the 1662 Book itself were of a static 'Christendom' England, so that little awareness of mission touches its pages; its requirements of the laity were of largely passive participation; and, for all its ancient beauties, its liturgical structuring has been called heavily into question in Province after Province and by scholars, pastors, and worshippers alike. There is inevitable pain for those who for perhaps half a century have found the approach to God through a well-loved pattern of language, and who then find it removed from them almost literally within a single night. But once a general direction of change is set, the transition, however painful, is better undertaken than evaded. Changes to modern idiom are not in fact confined in our Communion to liturgical English, but there are parallels, with a parallel transition, in at least one or two other languages.

Flexibility in Rites

186. Another traditional feature of Anglican rites is their fixedness and even rigidity. We seek now a far greater freeedom, which has ;its own marks of the Spirit. Whilst a set liturgy properly provides a ground-plan structure and the text of central prayers, yet nowadays it can and should often provide for material written for the occasion, for extemporary contributions, and for singing of items (whether time-honoured hymns or more instant choruses) chosen spontaneously. Provinces should be ready to have basic authorized forms for the central parts of certain rites such as the Eucharist, and for those forms to give a substantial part to the congregation. But they should also provide outline structures into which a choice of materials, already existent or written for the occasion, can be fitted. And we look for further openness still which will encourage the truly spontaneous contributions of spiritually alive congregations. (See Resolution 47).

Paragraph 184 comes to terms with facts. In essence there are two facts: firstly, the inevitable disappearance of 1662 where English is the main language of worship; and, secondly, its greater persistence in languages where the text is not archaic as it is in English, and (as in East and West Africa) where there has consequently been little informed criticism of it, or will to change it. Whilst even in the latter case there is a slow replacement of 1662 going on (and this Statement's concern for thorough inculturation might hasten that), yet in the former case, the use of 1662 (or, say, the American 1928 Book) is almost at an end. The Lambeth bishops were picketed by the (English) Prayer Book Society—but it has to be said that the bishops of the liturgy group, from all the English-speaking parts, could not conceive of their respective Prayer Book Societies as anything other than unrealistic and out of touch with the mission of the Church and the need for true renewal of its worship.

Paragraph 185 sets out more fully some of the reasons why 1662 does not well serve the mission of the Church to-day—reasons over and above the datedness and stained-glass-window character of Cranmer's liturgical prose. It is true that modern rites do not automatically make a congregation missionary or outward-looking, and certainly do not necessarily 'fill the Churches' (a prospectus never issued by writers of modern liturgy—but one on which they are sometimes thought to have first based their labours and then later defaulted . . .). But modern rites do cater for congregations open to the future, and optimistic under God about that future—whereas 1662 is so often treasured by those who are afraid of the future. The last part of the paragraph is therefore pastorally sensitive to those who are afraid. And the final sentence (which includes reference at least to Spanish and Portuguese) is a reminder that Anglicanism and English-speaking are not to be equated—a point made very clear during the Conference in the section discussions on the group's draft.

Paragraph 186 depicts a changing understanding of the written authorized texts. There was always an anomaly in these, in that in the past prayers had to be printed as part of the worship book, were treated as doctrinally normative, and were only varied under suspicion of grave disloyalty or even canonical disobedience—whereas hymnody was of no doctrinal standing whatsoever, and could be added almost anywhere and could say almost anything within the liturgy. There is a move in modern liturgy towards the 'Directory' style of presenting material—that is, that there is a ground-plan (or alternative ground-plans) for the structure of a worship event, and then very varied materials can be brought into that structure for the purpose of penitence, praise or petition. Many authorized Prayer Books of the last ten years show strong trends in this direction. But the paragraph is also urging the responsible use of materials written for a particular occasion, and also of wholly extemporary contributions. Whilst much of what is set out here would fulfil a charismatic programme, its intended purview is far wider and is about the coming alive of liturgy 'across the board'. Congregations are to participate actively, and to contribute from their own personal experience and understanding of the faith. The final cross-reference to Resolution 47 (for which see page 24 below) was added by the editors, but properly imports the inculturation dimension also.

Modern Liturgical English

187. A modern liturgical English is emerging. For somewhat more than twenty years worshippers have used texts which have abandoned 'thou' and address God as 'you'. A simpler more contemporary English has inevitably accompanied the change. We commend this, and welcome the efforts by first the International Consultation on English Texts (ICET) and more recently by the English Language Liturgical Consultation (ELLC) to find modern texts for 'common forms' which can be shared by all English-speaking countries across all the denominations. We recognize that ambiguous generic terms, such as 'man', 'men', and 'mankind', which arise through accidents of the English language rather than through anything ultimate or divine, have caused hurt to many as they touch deep emotions. We welcome the coming of 'inclusive' language.

Language about God

188. The question of using masculine terminology for God is treated more fully in paragraphs 77 and 78. Questions have been raised in some parts of the Communion as to whether such terminology has not been too dominant in our liturgical formulations. Some modern texts have found ways of softening it without eliminating it or raising doubts over it. However, even to raise the question would be inappropriate in other cultural contexts, and in the face of some other faiths. Even where it is raised, it provokes fundamental questions about the nature of the scriptural revelation, its particularity as well as its universality.

Simplicity of Language

189. We are also aware of a need emerging in some parts of our Communion of a simpler style of liturgical language, language which, nevertheless, retains the essential poetic and memorable character of good liturgical writing, and in its content still conveys the word of God. It need not always have great marks of permanence upon it, nor seek the weightiest provincial authorization. It may be sufficient that its provisionality and trial character enable it to be used for a period. And what is true of spoken texts is the more so of hymnody, songs, and choruses.

Contemporary materials will often enable worshippers to learn and maintain their faith through the character of what they say and sing, rather than through their ability to follow the printed page.

Non-Verbal Sharing in Liturgy

190. If we are not to be in captivity to a wholly 'word' and wholly 'book' liturgical culture, then we need to encourage communication by the visual and other senses, and to provide for congregational participation by action, gesture, movement and ceremonial. This should be such as to underline and reinforce the Word of God rather than to indicate a departure from it. A more uninhibited style of participation would be needed than has been usual amongst many Anglicans.

Silence

191. Our commendation of new styles of writing and of full congregational participation is not intended to subvert the role of silence in liturgy. Quite the reverse—the very liturgies which encourage active congregational responsiveness depend in their character upon silence structured alongside the activity. Anglicans generally should be ready for more of this arising from the very nature of the liturgy, and to be profitably used by the worshippers.

Paragraph 187 necessarily stops on the 'modern English' question, and, just as paragraph 186 sets the contrast with the fixedness of the 1662 concept of liturgy, so this paragraph sets the contrast of styles of English (concerning which paragraph 184 gave a broad hint). The actual watershed in the use of English seems to be the replacing of 'thou' with 'you' for the address to God. The 'thou' and 'you' indicator almost inevitably groups texts into ancient or modern categories.[1]

Hard on the heels of the form of address to God has come the issue of English pronouns and generic terms about us. It looks as though, after some fairly stressful internal struggle, the Anglican Communion is abandoning the generic use of 'man' and 'men'. The matter has dawned at different rates in different countries, so that it did not affect the production of the Church of England's ASB in 1978-79, nor the Church of Ireland's *Alternative Prayer Book* in 1983-84; but it was running strong in the USA in the early 1970s, and comes to a consistent conclusion in the Canadian *Book of Alternative Services* (1985) and the new New Zealand Prayer Book which gained final authorization in May 1988.

Paragraph 188 moves the discussion on from a point of change of terminology which the group could accept to one which the group could not. To cease talking about 'loving and serving all men' is one thing—to decline to use masculine pronouns about God is another. Paragraphs 77 and 78 further open the issue of the scriptural revelation mentioned here.

An example of the kind of 'softening' to which this paragraph refers is the use in the Canadian *Book of Alternative Services* of 'Let us give thanks to the Lord our God / It is right to give *our* thanks and praise'. Beyond that are far more speculative terms like 'God, the Father and Mother of us all', and the reflexive 'Godself'. The group, supported by the section, did not contemplate trying to walk, however cautiously, down that slippery slope.

Paragraph 189 reflects an awareness of a changed sociology of Anglicanism. Whereas the background expectation had always been that the Church of England, and its overseas offspring, belonged to the people, in fact its style of liturgy has been very literary and, whilst second nature to the believing literate and literati, has often seemed culturally far adrift from the less intellectual members of society, such as to constitute a barrier to their ever joining the fellowship. In England the report *Faith in the City* has further precipitated the quest for worship materials which will conform to the principles set out here. It is a new, and fascinating, task for commissions to attempt.

Paragraph 190 is one corrective to any misunderstandings introduced by lengthy discussion of language. We worship as whole people, and with our whole selves, which has been well established in paragraph 183. This recaptures that point—and both steers the puritans into an open-ness to more gesture and ceremonial than has been welcome to them hitherto, and perhaps also steers the anglo-catholic off a rigid commitment to an inherited pattern of ceremonialism, if that does not serve the present liturgical needs. Charismatics will take heart from the final sentence—all of us are being summoned to lose our self-consciousness in worship.

Paragraph 191 is a further corrective to any imbalance produced by the paragraphs on spoken texts. It insists that it is generally the modern liturgies, not the ancient ones, which write in rubrical provision for silence. That does not mean that modern users of liturgy have yet got the point, or understand how integral to a liturgical structure provision for silence may be.

[1] A fuller tracing of this trend is to be found in Colin Buchanan (ed.) *Anglican Eucharistic Liturgy 1975-1985* (Grove Books, 1985) pp.5-7, 24-27

Baptism
192. Baptism by water is the scriptural sacrament of once-for-all initiation into Christ and into his Body. The New Testament imagery displays a great spectrum of significance, from union with Christ in his death and resurrection, to incorporation by the Spirit into the one Body. The Church has always marked this life-changing step with vows expressing repentance and faith, the basic constituents of a response to the Gospel. The actual demands of repentance, and the Church's assessment of whether profession of it is genuine or not, will depend upon the specific needs and character of the social and religious context. All that is involved in being Christian is signified in baptism— God through baptism calls upon those who receive it to walk in his paths by the power of the Holy Spirit all the days of their lives.

The Baptism of Infants
193. We re-affirm the baptism of infants as scriptural, deriving in principle from the missionary baptism of households (e.g. Acts 16.15,33), a practice exemplified to-day in parts of our Communion. The baptism of infants shares as fully in the character of the one baptism as the baptism of adults, but we accept the Lima judgment that indiscriminate infant baptism should not be practised. It obscures the purpose of such baptism, not only from those who request it, but also from those many others who are doubtful about its propriety. Whilst we are aware of the vastly differing contexts in which baptism is sought, we encourage the development of standards and guidelines for the preparation of parents and sponsors, with a view to a common discipline.

Admission to Communion
194. The argument that baptism should in principle lead into sharing in communion has been strongly expressed in the call of the Boston Statement (1985).[27] The statement asks Provinces to cease to require confirmation, or any given standard of educational or other attainment, as a post-baptismal prerequisite for admission to communion. ACC-7 in May 1987 recorded in *Many Gifts, One Spirit* the situation in various Provinces.[28] This may indicate the likely future directions which are emerging in the Communion. The report also encouraged study of both the Lima Text and the Boston Statement (published as a separate eight-page pamphlet or contained within *Nurturing Children in Communion: Essays from the Boston Consultation)*[29], whilst raising its own questions over the latter. These questions range from concern about 'unworthy reception' (1 Corinthians 11.27f.) and the need for repentance to questions about the relation of baptism, as a complete rite of initiation, to a public profession of faith in the presence of the bishop, representing the wider Church. We recommend that the text of the Boston Statement and the ACC questions put to it should be widely circulated throughout our Communion, and a careful study made by Provinces which have not so far considered it. We judge that Provinces should be free to provide their own rules for the admission of the baptized to communion. Where two Provinces (or smaller units) have differing patterns, great sensitivity is needed where young children admitted to communion under one discipline then present themselves as communicants where a different discipline obtains.

[27] This Statement emerged from an International Consultation of a number of Anglican liturgists, the first of a series of such Consultations, which was held in Boston, Massachusetts, USA, from 29 to 31 July 1985.

[28] p.68f.

[29] Colin Buchanan (ed.) (Grove Books, Nottingham, 1985).

Paragraphs 192 to 201 handle a cluster of questions about sacramental initiation—all of them live in many parts of the Communion, and often troubling worshippers considerably. Whilst detailed discussion is impossible in this compass, and the section showed some nervousness lest traditional confirmation was being undercut in some of the drafting, yet in general the paragraphs together set out coherent principles.

Paragraph 192 itself simply sets the scene with a brief theological statement. The statements (like those of the Reformers) are intended to have universal applicability, whether adult or infant candidates are in view.

Paragraph 193 moves to the first particularity—the baptism of infants. It is insufficient to ground infant baptism on tradition alone especially if, as Baptists would frequently assert, the scriptures appear to deny that. Rather, a more careful examination of the scriptures themselves is needed, and infant baptism, if it can be grounded at all, must be grounded *there*. Hints as to that grounding are given, and, it will be noticed, infant baptism is derived not so much from a historical development from adult baptism, as from a separation from adult baptism in what was originally in essence 'household baptism'. There is of course a *logical* priority to the baptism of adults as it is parents who qualify children for baptism, but theological discussion and liturgical drafting must hold both categories closely together.

The fact that it is theologically parents who qualify their children for baptism leads inevitably to a consideration of the limits of the use of infant baptism. In England itself, not only was baptism open to all infants at the reformation time, but the clergy were supposed to hunt out any unbaptized, and were themselves to be disciplined if they failed to do so. As the transition has occurred in Western Europe from 'Christendom' to 'missiondom', so, even among pedo-baptists, grave doubts have arisen about 'indiscriminate baptism'. In other parts of the world, 'Christendom' never existed, or only had a pale shadow of its European character, and therefore no automatic expectation of the baptism of all-comers usually existed—it was only believing parents who would qualify their children for baptism.[1] Even practices which only *appear* to be indiscriminate, for all that their practitioners can cite some hidden principle by which they claim to operate, fall under the Lima judgment. The Lambeth Statement echoes this—implying that many who reject infant baptism have only seen its indiscriminate use, and its meaning and purpose have therefore been obscured from them. A dawning consciousness of the need to be careful about how widely infant baptism is administered opens the way for attempts at parochial, diocesan, or national guidelines.[2]

Paragraph 194 was perhaps the most 'worked over' of all the paragraphs. The enthusiasm of the group to air the 'Boston' principles was checked by an irrationality at the section which feared lest confirmation was being undermined (always a matter of concern to Anglican bishops).[3]

[1] *Baptism, Eucharist and Ministry* (WCC, Geneva, 1982) p.6. The Lima text which is quoted says: 'In order to overcome their differences, believer baptists and those who practise infant baptism should reconsider certain aspects of their practices. The first may seek to express more visibly the fact that children are placed under the protection of God's grace. The latter must guard themselves against the practice of apparently indiscriminate baptism and take more seriously their responsibility for the nurture of baptized children to mature commitment to Christ.'

[2] On the English scene, my *Policies for Infant Baptism* (Grove Worship Series 98, Grove Books, Bramcote, 1987) may be helpful—and General Synod is currently handling a Private Member's Motion on the subject.

[3] It was the editors, *not* the Lambeth bishops, who added the details of the ACC 'questions' *without* providing an equal summary of the Boston reasoning. This is extraordinary. See also Resolution 69 on p.24 below, and the Commentary on it.

Worship for All Ages

195. A corollary of infant baptism is that the main worship events of the Church should in principle be open to children. We should value their presence, treat their participation as natural, and ensure that the contents and ethos of the rite do not proclaim a spoken or silent message of rejection to them.

Confirmation of those Baptized in Infancy

196 The confirmation of those baptized as infants is by the laying on of the bishop's hands with prayer. In some cases it comes after admission to communion. The rite should include the first and major reaffirmation by the candidate of his or her baptismal covenant, prayer by the Church for a renewal of the baptismal life in the Spirit, and recognition by the Church of the candidate's adult participation in the mission of the Church.

Baptism of Adults

197. We judge that there is a growing proportion of adult candidates for baptism in our Communion, as compared with infants. We also note a slowly rising interest in some Provinces in the use of total immersion for such baptisms.[30] We also detect a widespread (though far from universal) expectation that the bishop will preside in person over the baptismal liturgy for adults (and for infants also where possible). The confirmation of those baptized in infancy (and the renewal of baptismal vows of others) fits well with the ritual for baptism itself. We welcome these trends.

The Laying on of Hands After the Baptism of Adults

198. The baptism of adults has since 1662 generally been followed by the laying on of hands by the bishop. Whilst questions have been raised recently about this, two clear patterns are to be found thus far in our Communion:

(i) The 1662 Prayer Book tradition is that an adult is baptized by the local pastor, perhaps at an early stage after professing faith, or sometimes on the eve of the bishop's visit to administer confirmation. This practice continues in many places.

(ii) A more recent development has been to combine adult baptism with confirmation in a single rite over which the bishop presides. This is found in many new rites of the last two decades.

Preparation

199. Just as we urge thorough preparation of parents for the baptism of an infant, so all the more we recommend thorough preparation of both candidate and sponsors at the baptism of an adult. Because it is entry into the missionary Body of Christ, baptism should lead, through the supportive fellowship of the Church, to a maturing process in the Spirit and to a sharing of Christ's ministry of service to the world. We note and commend a widespread interest in the revival of an adult catechumenate, and invite Provinces to consider the provision of guidelines for this.

---

[30] Such a practice is also known as baptism by *submersion.*

Paragraph 195 follows closely on the heels of Paragraph 194. Those who baptize infants ought to be asserting that thereafter full participation in worship is offered to believing children as they grow, and they are to *feel* included. Within the drafting group it was very clear that the end of the Paragraph spelled out in almost total transparency that children of believers should (along with other full participation) also be recipients of the sacrament of the eucharist with their parents. It may be that not all members of the section spotted this! Yet it has a very clear logic.

Paragraph 196 is simply descriptive, and is included partly because it is regular for Anglicans to discuss confirmation in connection with 'initiation', and partly because the statement originally needed a backdrop for the more difficult issue of confirmation after adult baptism. It will be clear that the Paragraph views Anglican confirmation as in essence a rite given, probably on the threshold of adulthood, to those baptized in infancy. Its rationale includes nothing which is itself formally sacramental, and nothing which either grounds the rite in Holy Scripture, or makes it an integral part of initiation, or treats it as of requirement for admission to communion.[1]

Paragraph 197 reflects the slow dying away of 'Christendom', and the sense of an evangelism to be fulfilled in both 'old' Christian areas as well as in 'new' areas of mission. 'Dipping' of candidates (best represented by the word 'submersion' which the drafters put in the text before the editors dropped it to a footnote) is the first option in both the 1662 Book (where it came from the first time) and in modern rites. Anglicans are distinguishable here not only by teaching that dipping is not essential, but also by a three-fold dipping when it is practised, whereas Baptists tend to submerge but once!

Paragraph 198 comes to the trickier question. In the days of a 'Mason-Dix' view of confirmation, as completing a two-stage sacramental initiation progress, revisers started to unite adult baptism and confirmation, in ways still to be found in the ASB. But it should be noted that all discussion of the meaning of baptism and of being a baptized person or a baptized company, wherever else in the Lambeth statement it comes, always refers simply to water baptism. Paragraph 196 above leaves no room for a rationale which would make sense of confirmation when baptism is given to adults—and there is indeed neither rationale nor sense. So the group originally included reference to a *third* pattern—the omission of confirmation in such cases. And here arises the scandal—in the Canadian *The Book of Alternative Services* (1985) the requirement of the laying on of the bishop's hands has been removed, and the newly baptized go straight into communion without 'confirmation'.[2] This is simply the truth of the rubrics and text, but at Lambeth the bishops in the section *did not want to have to read about what the Canadians have done*. No, the group had to suppress it, and simply leave a hint about 'questions' being raised. Yes, they certainly are.

---

[1] See my *Anglican Confirmation* (Grove Liturgical Study no. 48, Grove Books, Bramcote, 1986) for a recent review of the relevant evidence.

[2] See *Book of Alternative Services* p.160. The only mandatory post-baptismal ceremony is the signing with the sign of the cross—and no-one could think that *that* is confirmation.

Testimony

200. We also recommend in a baptism and confirmation context, what Lambeth 1978 said in an evangelistic tone [*misprint for* 'one'], that there is great effectiveness in 'a personal word of testimony',[31] and we suggest provision for this in the rites of our Communion.

Re-Affirmation of Baptismal Vows

201. Because baptism is once-for-all and for life, it cannot be repeated and, once given, must not be denied. We commend experiments with the re-affirmation of the baptismal covenant over and above confirmation, and, provided that the givenness of earlier baptism itself is not obscured or threatened, we recognize the possibilities of such reaffirmation being accompanied by appropriate meaningful ceremonies. One such possible ceremony is the laying on of hands, which is provided in at least two recent Worship Books in a way which is clearly distinguished from traditional confirmation.[32]

Rites of Reconciliation

202. Whilst rites of reconciliation of a penitent may be regularly used for Christians in all patterns of life, we also see a case, closely allied to the rite of re-affirmation of the baptismal covenant, as set out in paragraph 199 [*misprint for* '201'] above, for a special and public restoration of those who, once baptized (and indeed also confirmed), are now returning from being 'lapsed' and are best welcomed in this public way.

Eucharist: Meeting and Mission

203. We do not attempt here to discuss textual technicalities of the eucharistic rites. Instead we note that in the eucharist the Church unites in the praises of God, receives God's holy word, expresses her life in the Spirit, sustains the mutual fellowship of her members, re-commits herself to Almighty God, and, from this holy feast, returns to the world to fulfil God's mission. The eucharist is a locus for mutual sharing and ministry for the 'building up' of the Church (1 Cor. 14). The eucharist may include: various teaching methods to minister the word, drama, dance, extemporary prayer, groups for study or intercession, healing ministries, weddings, and other public activities of the local Christian community. Christian mission itself is vitiated if the Church's eucharistic practice does not in fact build up the people of God.

The Agape

204. We note signs of the re-emergence of the *agape* or love feast. It appears in two forms; eucharistic, in the sense of having the sacrament of the Lord's Supper at its heart, or non-eucharistic, though still with elements of Christian worship within it. It is interesting to note that, in its non-eucharistic form, it is often used by local groups of Christians, in the absence of a duly ordained minister.[33]

---

[31] *Report*, p.94.

[32] E.g. *The Book of Common Prayer* of the Episcopal Church, USA (Church Hymnal Corporation, New York, 1979) and *The Book of Alternative Services* of the Anglican Church in Canada (Anglican Book Centre, Toronto, 1985).

[33] Leonardo Boff, *Ecclesio-Genesis* (Collins, London, 1986) pp.61f.

Paragraph 200 echoes brave words of Lambeth 1978, and takes them into the liturgical pattern for initiation. There are two ways in which this use of public testimony in pastoral logic actually precedes the deliberately evangelistic use: firstly, if a candidate for baptism is asked *why* he or she desires baptism, and then has to answer publicly in an individual way related to his or her actual experience of coming to faith, then that personal testimony underlines and reinforces the meaning and solemnity of the baptismal reprentance and faith—and contains a divine stimulus also to all those present; and, secondly, if the candidate ever is going to testify in the future to perhaps hostile unbelievers, then to be able to do so in the more sympathetic company of the faithful, *right from the moment of baptism* (or at least of confirmation) is a great step in the right direction.

Paragraph 201 is the final part of the 'baptismal' drafting. Whilst confirmation has always been the place for 'set-piece' re-affirmation (or ratification) of baptismal declarations, recent years have shown a great need for further re-affirmations for those already confirmed. The two Worship Books mentioned (see footnote 32) provide three different parallel understandings of post-baptismal re-affirmations of baptismal faith—confirmation itself (see Paragraph 196); re-affirmation for those being restored (especially in view here); and the reception of communicants of other denominations (whether Roman Catholic or non-episcopal) without the requirement of confirmation *simpliciter.* The more radical, yet more logical, 'meaningful ceremony' for re-affirmation would be the re-application of water. Quite apart from Easter Eve ceremonies, there exists in many places a desire by some to re-affirm their baptismal vows by receiving either pouring or submersion (though Anglicans would always have to distinguish such rites from baptism *ab initio*). The group could not agree whether or how to state this, and left it unsaid—but some members are well aware of a pastoral need of tried models for this.

Paragraph 202, whilst it is closely related to both 'baptismal' and 're-affirmation' liturgical provision, relates to a matter usually treated as separate from them. The provision in some modern revisions of rites entitled 'The Reconciliation of a Penitent' could lead us towards private confession and absolution—but it is the churchly dimension which is emphasized by a link with public re-affirmation of the baptismal covenant, and it is given expression in, for example, the instances quoted at the end of Paragraph 201 above.

Paragraphs 203 and 204 touch briefly on the eucharist. Their great concern is to locate the eucharist at the heart of the Church's mission, giving distinctive identity to the people of God, and equipping them for their pilgrimage and witness in the world. On a full understanding of mission, the eucharist should model that joining in love which we covet for all society, and for which our liturgical practice ought to be an eschatological anticipation. The original drafting centred round the concept of 'meeting' (note the Paragraph heading), but the editors omitted this word. The 'agape' suggestion is itself a fuller expression of love, and requires a much deeper engagement of the participants with each other than a poker-faced eucharistic celebration may of itself do.[1]

---

[1] There are passing references to it in rubrics in the ECUSA *Book of Common Prayer,* in the eucharistic liturgy of the Church of North India, and elsewhere. There is larger provision and guidance (almost to the point of menus!) in the Church of England's *Lent Holy Week Easter* services. See also Trevor Lloyd, *Celebrating the Agape To-Day* (Grove Worship Series no. 97, 1986).

Presidency at the Eucharist

205. We note the received tradition that the president of the eucharist should be a bishop or presbyter. We also note that in dioceses which are geographically large, or offer grave hindrances to easy travel, the ready availability of an ordained presbyter may not match the proper sacramental hopes or expectations of some or all of the congregations. Two practices have found acceptance in some parts of our Communion:

(i) the ordination of local persons—who are acknowledged leaders in the congregation or congregations, but who may lack some of the traditional requirements for ordination. Such people can then provide the presidency required at the eucharist, in addition to their other roles in the Church.

(ii) the 'extending' of communion through space and time by the hands of specially authorized lay persons (or deacons) who take the elements from a normal celebration (with a presbyter or bishop presiding) to needy individuals and congregations.

Distribution of Communion

206. No important principles are breached if authorized lay persons of either sex minister either element to the communicants. In some situations, indeed, it is more appropriate to pass the elements along rows of worshippers than to administer to each individually.

Non-Eucharistic Worship

207. We look for the emergence of richer forms of non-eucharistic worship throughout the Communion. We note particularly the need for the development of offices, particularly where a simple, daily, lay office is desired; family services, particularly for those on the fringe of Church life and commitment; liturgies for informal groups, such as bible study groups or adult enquirers' classes; and material for ecumenical worship particularly for use with those with whom we cannot share communion. The principles of such worship need to be articulated afresh and specific models need to be worked out.

Lectionary

208. We note the call of Lambeth 1978 for a 'common lectionary' both as a unifying factor within the Communion and for use ecumenically.[34] We urge, once again, that everything possible should be done to reach an agreement on such a lectionary.

Ordination

209. The 1958 Lambeth Conference Report, while drawing attention to some deficiencies in the 1662 Ordinal, particularly emphasized the centrality of *prayer* as the 'form' of the ordination rite. Most revisions of the last thirty years, stemming from valuable work in the Church of South India, are based on this insight. We believe they should be more acceptable to the worldwide Communion and to our ecumenical partners. We know of no doubtful revisions. It is perhaps an area where very careful co-ordination of provincial revisions is vital. We recommend that all Provinces should study the character of these revised rites with a view to the emergence of a common mind in this matter. (See Resolution 18.6c)

[34] *Report*, p.47.

Paragraph 205 went back and forth between group and section. At the first encounter a South American bishop urged us to include discussion of lay presidency—a logical third option, and one much favoured by Anglicans in some parts of the Southern Cone. The group duly drafted a cautious reference to the *possibility* of the solution, but were then told to take it out. The group's own discernment was that the general Anglican way of dealing with the issue is to try *to ensure that it is not debated;* it is doubtful whether the issue will simply go away . . .

Of the two solutions mentioned, 'extended communion' is nowadays a much less contentious issue than years ago – a matter helped by the diminishing of the 'cultus', so that 'reserving' is truly directed to the actual needs of real people, who are ill or otherwise cut off from the eucharist. The 'local ordained ministry' issue has implications which are not strictly 'worship' ones. Neither solution always meets the actual needs of remote villages, currently visited by a presbyter (a term the group preferred to 'priest') at, say, two-monthly intervals. Anglicans must often be ready for a (largely) non-sacramental way of life to be established and honoured—and, of course, the Southern Cone issue exists in many other places also.

Paragraph 206 will seem not worth mentioning in many places, but in England (where persons of either sex may administer either element with the bishop's permission) many still speak as though only Readers could 'assist with the cup'—and at the Conference itself there was a minor unhappiness from overseas when it was discovered that laypeople, including women, were helping distribute both elements—when presbyters, let alone bishops galore, were present in large quantitities . . . (Do not put distributants into choir habit or other ecclesiastical vesture—let them come as they are.)

Paragraph 207 sets out agenda on a grand scale in a small compass. All round the Anglican Communion there is a sense that traditional 'daily offices' are over-formal for daily use, and over-restrictive for much Sunday use—and therefore all kinds of innovation or creative borrowing are needed.

Paragraph 208 deals with a well-known feature of the world liturgical scene—the Roman Catholic three-year lectionary, which is in use in many Anglican Churches (e.g. Australia), and is viewed as *the* 'common lectionary' in America. However, in Britain the two-year ecumenical lectionary was in existence before the Roman Catholic one was issued, and it has persisted here and elsewhere. In 1983-84 the General Synod of the Church of England debated a report comparing the two lectionaries, and declined to authorize the Roman Catholic one. To that extent the bishops from Britain must be viewed as no more than luke-warm about a 'common lectionary'.

Paragraph 209 arises from an awareness that ordination rites are part of the ecumenical agenda (especially, of course, *vis a vis* Rome).[1] There was also discussion of such rites in another sub-group and they in two paragraphs (175 and 176) deal with a study of ordination rites, and the editors did not stitch the two sets of material together.

[1] The new Anglican rites of the lat forty years, with some of their ancestry, are set out in my *Modern Anglican Ordination Rites* (Alcuin/GROW Joint Liturgical Study, Grove Books, 1987). This displays the ordination prayers in particular, and also the post-ordination ceremonies, whilst summarizing details of the presentation of candidates, the interrogation, the intercessions, and the eucharistic material.

5. RESOLUTIONS BEARING UPON LITURGY

18. The Anglican Communion: Identity and Authority

[PARAS 1-5 concern internal relationships of the Anglican Communion and the role to be fulfilled by the varrious inter-Anglican organs.]

6. [This Conference] Requests the Archbishop of Canterbury, with all the Primates of the Anglican Communion, to appoint an Advisory Body on Prayer Books of the Anglican Communion. The Body should be entrusted with the task of offering encouragement, support and advice to Churches of the Communion in their work of liturgical revision as well as facilitating mutual consultation concerning, and review of, their Prayer Books as they are developed with a view to ensuring:

   (a) the public reading of the Scriptures in a language understood by the people and instruction of the whole people of God in the scriptural faith by means of sermons and catechisms;

   (b) the use of the two sacraments ordained by Christ, baptism with water in the threefold Name, and Holy Communion with bread and wine and explicit intention to obey our Lord's command;

   (c) the use of the forms of episcopal ordination to each of the three orders by prayer with the laying-on of hands;

   (d) the public recitation and teaching of the Apostles' and Nicene Creeds; and

   (e) the use of other liturgical expressions of unity in faith :and life by which the whole people of God is nurtured and ;upheld, with continuing awareness of ecumenical liturgical developments.

22. Christ and Culture

This Conference

(a) Recognizes that culture is the context in which people find their identity.

(b) Affirms that God's love extends to people of every culture and that the Gospel judges every culture according to the gospel's own criteria of truth, challenging some aspects of culture while endorsing others for the benefit of the Church and the society.

(c) Urges the Church everywhere to work at expressing the unchanging Gospel of Christ in words, actions, names, customs, liturgies, which communicate relevantly in each contemporary society.

23. Freedom of Religious Activity

This Conference calls upon all governments to uphold religious freedom, including freedom of worship and freedom to teach and evangelize, as a fundamental human right, the denial of which threatens all other liberties.

47. Liturgical Freedom

This Conference resolves that each Province should be free, subject to essential universal Anglicans norms of worship, and to a valuing of traditional liturgical materials, to seek that expression of worship which is appropriate to its Christian people in their cultural context.

60. Recognition of Saints

This Conference

1. Welcomes the proposal by Africa Region that the Anglican Communion should recognize men and women who have lived godly lives as saints by including them in the calendars of the Churches for remembrance; and

2. Recommends that the Anglican Consultative Council discusses this matter and advises the Provinces on the procedure to follow in recognition of such saints.

69. Admission to Communion

This Conference requests all Provinces to consider the theological and pastoral issues involved in the admission of those baptized but unconfirmed to communion (particularly as set out in the Report of ACC-7), and to report their findings to the ACC.